WHEN DRAG IS NOT A CAR RACE

AN IRREVERENT DICTIONARY OF OVER 400 GAY AND LESBIAN WORDS AND PHRASES

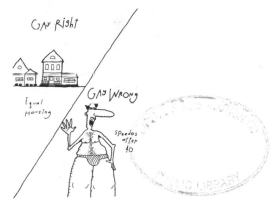

Gay Right

Equal Housing

Gay Wrong

Speedos after 40

JEFF FESSLER AND KAREN RAUCH
Illustrated by Jeff Fessler

A FIRESIDE BOOK · PUBLISHED BY SIMON & SCHUSTER

To Dad—whom I consider the source of my sense of humor.
—KR

To Ron Romanovsky and Paul Phillips for proving how well
the arts and activism go hand in hand.
—JF

FIRESIDE
Rockefeller Center
1230 Avenue of the Americas
New York, NY 10020

FIRESIDE and colophon are registered trademarks
of Simon & Schuster Inc.

Designed by Bonni Leon-Berman

Manufactured in the United States of America

1   3   5   7   9   10   8   6   4   2

Library of Congress Cataloging-in-Publication Data

Fessler, Jeff.
When drag is not a car race : an irreverent dictionary of over 400
gay and lesbian words and phrases / Jeff Fessler and Karen Rauch :
illustrated by Jeff Fessler.
p.   cm.
"A Fireside book."
1. Homosexuality—Dictionaries.   2. Lesbianism—Dictionaries.
3. Homosexuality—Humor.   4. Lesbianism—Humor.
I. Rauch, Karen.   II. Title.
HQ75.17.F47   1997   97-11165
306.76'6'03—dc21   CIP

ISBN 0-684-83081-7

Contents

Acknowledgments

We thank the creative and humorous minds of Dr. Alina Alonso, Reid Bratager, Ember Carianna, Lori Haynes, Jane Hutton, Bob Klekner, Billy Pace, Mike Sand, Chris Scholl, Michael Sovis, Nancie Vollmer, Scott Wade, Kathy Wall, Jamey Young, and all those helpful eggheads on the Internet.

Preface

Noah Webster, America's primo dictionary guy, sought to give American English a certain dignity of its own. He disliked the common, taboo words of his day and often commented on the vulgarity of the jargon in Samuel Johnson's 1755 *Dictionary of the English Language*.

So as you read our dictionary, realize that the rumbling sounds you hear are Mr. Webster violently rolling over in his grave. While our dictionary has a certain dignity of its own, it is often a vulgar, taboo type of dignity. But you can bet your box, Miss Thang, that it's a lot more fun than anything old Noah ever penned.

Unlike Mr. Webster or Mr. Johnson we hardly consider ourselves authorities on any segment of the English language, homospeak included, but we did our best. We used the most comprehensive authorities on the subject (our friends) and even used the Internet to gather lingo nationwide.

However, we realize that what one considers "sassy" in Anchorage might very well be considered "tired" in Albuquerque. And undoubtedly there are at least five or ten more words for crotch. So if you know of a lesbian- or gay-related word, phrase, or acronym not included in our dictionary, e-mail us at dragbook@aol.com. Until then, grab a rail, girl. You're in for the most vulgar, dignified ride of your life!

1

Men on Men

GAY GUY TERMINOLOGY

AMW ActorModelWaiter (as in, "I'm an actor and model, but I'll get that order of potato skins in right away for you").

AUNTIE Old gay guy with a persona not unlike the *Andy Griffith Show*'s Aunt Bea: matronly, domestic, and creator of the best pecan pies this side of Mayberry.

BEAR Follicly gifted gay guy, with hair covering parts of the body you never thought possible. *Also:* teddy bear.

BENT 1. Early English term for gay guy. 2. Broadway play about gay prisoners in a German concentration camp that starred Richard Gere.

BIG GIRL Flamboyant, effeminate gay guy. *Also:* big woman.

BIRD Early 20th-century British slang for gay guy.

A BEAR (RIGHT)

BONA PALOME Gay cockney word for a hunk.

BUTT PIRATE Somewhat tacky, though swashbuckling, term for gay guy. *Also:* backdoor bandit.

BUTTERCUP 1930s floral-like slang for effeminate gay guy. Ironically, buttercup flowers are

When Drag Is Not a Car Race

also called crowfeet, a word gay guys have removed from their vocabulary.

BUTCH Marlboro Man–looking gay guy; masculinity plus. *Opposite:* femme.

CHICKEN Young gay guy, in the finger-lickin' good sense.

CHICKEN HAWK Older gay guy who prefers his dates young and tender. *See* CHICKEN.

CLONES In the 1970s and 1980s, gay guys who opted for the same pseudo-heterosexual look, including mustache, tight jeans, knit polo shirt, and short hair. This attempt to "fit in" created a scary army of replicants that became even more conspicuous.

CUB Youngish version of a bear; more of a Boo-Boo than a Yogi ("That 19-year old college boy I took to the beach turned out to be quite the cub. When he took off his shirt it was *I Was a Teenage Werewolf* all over again!").

CUCA South Beach gay guy term; pronounced KOO-kuh, from Spanish word for cockroach. Adopted due to similarities between Miami's cockroaches and South Beach gay guys: both are only seen at night, scurry in and out of dark places, and even if you only see one, you know there are hundreds more close by. Used endearingly, never as an insult ("That's such a cuca outfit Manuel!").

DADDY Masculine, older dominant guy. Father figure, indeed. *Also:* sugar daddy (wealthy). ("Either Chip is taking his grandfather to a movie or he's snagged another sugar daddy.")

DECOR-INA Sort of like a ballerina, but does interiors instead of dance steps.

DRAG 1. When a guy dresses like a woman, or a woman dresses like a guy. 2. When a lesbian or gay person wears clothing unlike his or her normal attire—that is, when a butch lesbian wears a dress, when a conservative gay guy wears all leather.

DRAG QUEEN A guy who dresses like a woman and who has achieved diva status like RuPaul (NOTE: not every guy who dresses like a gal is worthy of "drag queen" status); often performs professionally by lip-synching popular songs by female singers or by singing for real.

FAGGOT Gay guy (derogatory). Now often used in jest among gay guys. Possible origins: 1. Cigarettes were called fags in Britain during World War I and considered unmanly. 2. In the 1500s, disagreeable/objectionable women were called faggots as a term of abuse. 3. In the 1800s, English boarding schools had a system called fagging where lower classmen performed certain duties (including sexual) for upper classmen. 4. In medieval times homosexuals were executed by burning bundles of sticks (called faggots) under them. 5. A faggot was a sorcerer's wand used for divination and sacred firemaking, which was the province of gay wizards, sorcerers, and priests for thousands of years.

FAGGOTRESS Uppity queen who is a legend in his own mind, existing in a fantasy world of nobility—even though he works at the Caramel Corn stand at the mall.

FAIRY Pixielike, effeminate gay guy. Named after those tiny, imaginary, supernatural creatures who possess magic power and help/annoy humans.

FEMME Effeminate gay guy. *Opposite:* butch.

FLAMER Very effeminate, often overbearing gay guy ("I thought I smelled smoke—here comes that huge flamer Dennis").

FLAMER

FRIEND OF DOROTHY Older term for gay guy; refers to Dorothy from the *Wizard of Oz* (her friends weren't humans, but they sure were queens). Probably originated from gay guys' admiration for Judy Garland, supergoddess of the silver screen.

I want to get in his pants, but I don't have a wrench...

FRIEND OF DOROTHY

FRUIT Gay guy. *Also:* fruitcake, fruit of the loom (gay fashion designer), fresh fruit (very forward gay guy).

GWM Classified ad abbreviation for gay white male. *Also:* GBM (gay black male), GWF (gay white female), etc. ("GWM w/UPS seeks GBM @ CBS for R&R. Must like KFC, STP, IBM & AOL. Call ASAP.")

GIRL Tacked on to any sentence regardless of the gender to whom one speaks ("Girl, stay out of the rain or all that hairspray you have on will turn to lacquer!").

GIRLFRIEND How some gay guy pals refer to each other.

GLAMAZON When beauty and brawn collide; a statuesque enchantress who is once, twice, three times a lady—three times the height, three times the Chanel makeup, three times the Versace. Created by drag queen extraordinaire RuPaul.

GREY WOLF Older gay guy who likes his dates more on the pup side. And naturally, he's always hungry like the wolf.

GUNSEL 19th-century term derived from German and Yiddish, meaning a young, inexperienced gay guy.

HIT Homo in training; gay guy new to the scene. *Also:* trainee fag.

HOMO Short for homosexual. Once considered derogatory but often used in jest among lesbians and gays.

INVERT Early 20th-century slang for a gay guy; homosexuality was referred to as "sexual inversion."

LICKBOX Orally fixated, turn-of-the-century terminology for gay guy.

LIGHT IN THE LOAFERS Grandmotherly term for gay guy ("Uncle Fritz always said he bought those muscle magazines for the articles, but if you ask me he was a little light in the loafers").

LIZZIE Popular 1920s term for gay guy. Not to be confused with Lizzie Borden, axe murderess.

MARY Effeminate gay guy ("Look at him trying on eyeliner at the Lancôme counter . . . what a Mary!"). *Also:* Mary talk, the language of Marys.

MISS THING Snippy term for someone who has irritated you ("Listen Miss Thing, you talk one more time during *Melrose Place* and you'll be wearing that bean dip"). *Also:* Miss Thang.

MOLLY 1700s British term for gay guy. Derived from men's club The Mollies, whose members were known to be gay and were noted for their wild partying in women's clothing.

NANCY Early 20th-century slang for gay guy. Probably not derived from dyke-like cartoon character of the same name.

NELLIE Effeminate gay guy even your grandmother could figure out. Whoa, Nellie!

ORCHID EATER Seemingly bizarre term for gay guy, until one discovers that "orchid" derives from the Greek word for testicle.

PANSY Antiquated name for an affectedly proper gay guy, or the little flower with a big attitude. It's unnoticeable if alone, but ostentatious in bunches.

POWDER PUFF Jailhouse term for an effeminate man, usually the one who drops the bar of soap in the prison shower.

PRINCESS A queen in the making (just give him some time to grow bitter).

PUFF Cockney for gay guy. Not to be confused with the magic dragon of the same name whose sexual orientation is unknown.

PUNK African American term for gay guy.

PUTO Derogatory Latin American term for gay guy.

QUEEN Effeminate gay guy with a royal attitude. *Also:* evil queen—a really, really nasty queen ("I'm so tired of faggy little Emmett telling *me* how to act more masculine. He's a bigger queen than Beatrix!").

RFD QUEEN Rural free delivery queen; 1950s term for gay guy from the country. Hee haw!

REAL Homosexual ("Don't let Chester's tool belt and boot-cut Wrangler jeans fool you . . . he's as real as they come").

RETAIL QUEEN Queen with mall job for life.

ROUGH TRADE Hustler from the wrong side of the tracks.

SCARE QUEEN Really, really unattractive queen ("That scare queen over by the bar tried to strike up a conversation with me until his crypt breath drove me away!").

RETAIL QUEEN

SCREAMER 1. Extremely effeminate gay guy. 2. One who makes lovemaking a vocal event.

SHE He. Used when referring to gay guy, especially an effeminate guy ("Christopher is absolutely impossible! She is working my last gay nerve!").

SISSY Gay guy ("He may look like a stud, but there's a big ol' sissy underneath all those muscles").

SISTER Term of affection between gay guy pals ("Oh, no, Lester and I aren't boyfriends, just sisters").

SNOW QUEEN 1. Black queen who dates only white guys. 2. Gay guy who uses cocaine.

SWEATER QUEEN Prissy gay guy with exaggerated preppy overtones (you know the look: a sweater worn like a cape, its arms tied around the shoulders/neck. How "last decade"!). *Also:* sweater fag.

SWISH When a gay guy acts extremely effeminate; derives from the flamboyant body motions that cause his body parts to swish through the air ("Caesar has nerve swishing right into that straight club!").

TELEFAG Phone-addicted gay guy. Probably has cell phone, beeper, voice mail, and one of those headsets like Madonna wore on the Blonde Ambition tour.

TOMMY DODD Late Victorian slang for gay guy. *Also:* tommies (plural).

TROLL Older gay guy in desperate search for younger gay guy. Doesn't necessarily live under a bridge, but you never know.

TWINKIE Young, inexperienced gay guy/cream-filled snack.

URANIAN 1800s German slang for gay guy. Derived from German homosexual rights activist Karl Heinrich Ulrichs in 1862, who took the term from *Plato's Symposium,* in which homosexual love existed under the protection of the ninth muse, Urania. *Also:* urning.

2

Girls on Girls

LESBIAN TERMINOLOGY

Have drill, will travel

B & D DYKE

AMAZON Towering, powerful, aggressive woman, from the legendary South American tribe of female warriors ("That woman I went out with Saturday was such an Amazon! I might as well be dating Xena the Warrior Princess!").

B & D DYKE Black & Decker dyke; a Home Depot junkie who could give Bob Vila a run for his money. *Also:* bondage & discipline dyke. Thank you ma'am, may I have another!

BABY DYKE Young lesbian, just out/new to the scene.

BOWLER Lesbian; one who bowls—or wears shoes that make her look like she does ("That new attorney on the third floor is definite bowler material . . . she's an avid kayaker, has a belch that will hurt your eardrums, and get a load of those sensible shoes!").

BULL DYKE Lesbian who wears a wide leather belt with her girlfriend's name tooled in it and her keys hanging off of it. Probably unshaven, could probably beat the crap out of any man. *Also:* bull dagger.

BULL DYKE

BUTCH The lesbian who takes out the trash and does whatever else the femme tells her to do. She transgresses the traditional female role, but don't call her masculine!

CS Comfortable shoes; code for a potential lesbian sighting ("Darla, don't look now but that woman in front of us buying the four cans of Quaker State oil is definitely CS").

CARPET MUNCHER Floor-covering–inspired term for lesbian (derogatory). Whether it's shag or a tight weave, let's hope it's DuPont Stainmaster. *Also:* rug muncher.

CHICKEN *See* BABY DYKE.

CRONE Derogatory term for crusty, old lesbian. Derives from Middle English "croonie," meaning old ewe. B-a-a-a-a-hum-bug!

DIT Dyke in training; a lesbian who is new to the scene.

DWOM Dyke without money; gay shopkeeper term based on the stereotype that lesbians are penny-pinching tightwads who would rather create their clothes hangers from scrap wire than buy them at ten for a dollar.

DEMO DYKE Demonstrating/protesting/excruciatingly politically correct dyke ("Myrna is now boycotting any product produced by a male-owned company. The poor thing sits home, covered with Mary Kay cosmetics, gorging herself on Mrs. Paul's fish sticks").

DIESEL DYKE Very masculine lesbian; truck driver–like but meaner and smellier.

DYKE Lesbian; once considered a derogatory term but now used regularly by lesbians and gay men.

DYKES ON BIKES Lesbian motorcycle mamas. When they say they like something hot, solid, and vibrating between their legs, they aren't talking about a penis.

DYKES WITH MIKES Singing lesbians (for example, k.d. lang).

ELECTIVE LESBIAN Female who chooses to be a lesbian, rather than letting her genes choose for her ("Let's see, tonight I think I'll wear my red dress, my leather mules, and my lesbian personality").

FAIRY LADY 1950s term for a lesbian bottom, a female version of the male "fairy."

FEMME Feminine, passive lesbian who probably carries a purse and understands the importance of moisturizing.

FETCH AND CARRY DYKE In a relationship, the lesbian who does what she's told ("Honey, bring me my Meisterbräu and that bag of Chee·tos, on the double!").

GLAMOUR DYKE Lipstick lesbian with subscriptions to fashion magazines.

GRANOLA LESBIAN Earthy, tofu-eating, Birkenstock-wearing, you-make-me-feel-like-a-natural-woman kind of woman.

KI-KI Means "neither-nor," a 1950s lesbian term for a woman who does not consistently follow one role in bed (that is, butch/femme).

LABRYS Axe with double sides, sometimes used as lesbian power emblem.

LEATHER DYKE Cowhide-clad lesbian. Thank you, ma'am, may I have another!

LESBERADO A cross between a lesbian and a desperado (Myra moved in with some lesberado fresh out of the slammer—she always was a pushover for those women-in-prison films").

LESBIAN Homosexual woman. Term derives from Greek isle of Lesbos where Sappho, who wrote poetry about love between women, started a female school in 6 B.C.E.

LESBIAN SEPARATIST Lesbians who choose to deal only with women as much as possible ("Liz is such a separatist . . . she wouldn't let me take her picture in front of the Washington Monument because she said it looked like a big penis!").

LESBIAN THOUGHT POLICE Fanatical, self-appointed comptroller of conduct regarding all things lesbian, operating under the belief that all lesbians should be clonelike ("All I did was put on a little eyeliner and Ada gave me the lecture about how I am submitting to society's flawed concept of beauty that exploits women. Who died and made her captain of the lesbian thought police?").

LESBIAN SEPARATIST

LEZBO Lesbian, but usually shouted out of a car window by a group of redneck heterosexual men ("Hey Elmer, check out the lezbo with the pit bull!"). Derivation of Lesbos, Greek isle and birthplace of Sappho (although it's doubtful the rednecks have made this connection).

LEZZIE Lesbian (derogatory). Another redneck-inspired insult.

LIPSTICK LESBIAN Popular nineties term for feminine, makeup-wearing, bejeweled lesbian who shops for undergarments at Victoria's Secret (rather than Foot Locker).

LITTLE DUTCH BOY Lesbian. Derived from legend of Dutch boy who stuck his finger in a dike (you know, the other kind).

LUPPIES Lesbian yuppies ("A place in Aspen, a shiny Saab, and severely sensible shoes . . . those two gals next door have *got* to be luppies!").

MANNISH LESBIAN Turn-of-the-century term for woman defined as a lesbian because her behavior/dress included elements considered exclusively masculine (that is, wearing a man's top hat and jacket, hair clipped short and slicked back).

MANTEE Butch lesbian; strong enough for a man, but made for a woman.

MUFF DIVER Colorful term for lesbian; imagine a Jacques Cousteau–like plunge toward the genitals.

MUSCLE MARY Muscularly gifted lesbian usually in sleeveless shirts.

ROMANTIC FRIENDSHIP Polite, 1700s-era euphemism for lesbianism.

SAPPHO Lesbian; from the Greek poetess of the same name, born on the Isle of Lesbos.

SERGEANT 1950s terminology for a butch lesbian, probably originating from women involved in World War II.

SISTER Term of affection and camaraderie between lesbians. *Also:* sacred sisterhood.

SPINSTER An unmarried woman beyond the usual age for marrying. In the early 1900s, often used as a euphemism for old lesbian ("Your great aunt Irene was a sweet old spinster who never found a husband. It's amazing how many other spinsters she managed to befriend!").

STONE BUTCH The woman on top.

TOD Tired old dyke (that is, Maude).

TOMBOY A butch girl, often a euphemism for lesbian ("Mom, when will you tell your friends I'm a lesbian? It's getting harder to believe that tomboy explanation now that I'm over 47!").

TORTILLERA Not a new dish at Taco Bell, but Spanish for dyke, especially used in Cuba ("Lucy, I'm your husband . . . you can tell me. Are you and Ethel tortilleras?").

TRIBADE A woman who practices tribadism (lesbianism). Tribadism derives from the Greek word for rubbing. Rub-a-dub-dub, three dykes in a tub!

TURKEY BASTER BABY What the lesbian stork brings; child of a female couple conceived through at-home artificial insemination. Wash that thing out well before Thanksgiving!

VULVA HANDS Gang-like hand symbol that involves placing the thumbs and forefingers together to create a triangle that is held over the head. Probably used more at lesbian events than at, say, the mall or 7-Eleven.

WIMMIN Getting the "man" out of "woman"; often used by lesbian separatists. *Also:* wimyn.

WOMEN LOVING WOMEN Straightforward term for lesbians.

3

In, Out of, and Not Even Near the Closet

DESCRIPTIONS OF OURSELVES AND OTHERS

How much is this vase ma'am... um, I mean sir... no, uh....

AC-DC When your sexual current can go one way or the other; bisexual.

ALTERNATIVE Often a euphemism for homosexuality as in "alternative lifestyle" ("My brother's on his third marriage, my married cousin is sleeping with her boss, and my neighbor beats his wife once a week. And they call *my* lifestyle 'alternative' because I'm a lesbian!").

ANDROGYNOUS Gender challenged; an appearance that falls somewhere in between male and female.

BEARD Woman as accessory; a female who acts as a gay man's date at social functions, often for business purposes.

BI Bisexual; one who is attracted to both males and females.

BREEDER Heterosexual person (once derogatory, but less so now that lesbians and gays continue to become parents, via artificial insemination, adoption, etc. Call it the gay-bee boom!).

BEARD (CENTER)

BUNKER SHY Guy afraid of being forced into sex by one of those perverted, recruiting homosexuals. Probably originates from World War I term for a soldier afraid that the other GI sharing his bunker might make a sexual advance.

Doesn't everyone have sex on the mind in the throes of a bloody battle?

CHURCH MEMBER Homosexual person ("Bart may work that straight boy act, but I know he's a church member").

CLOSETED Homosexuals who keeps their sexual orientation secret. *Also:* in the closet.

COMING OUT Admitting to yourself/your family/ the world that you are homosexual. *Also:* coming out of the closet ("What do you mean 'have I come out to my family'? I brought my boyfriend as my date to my sister's bat mitzvah!").

CONFUSED Lesbian/gay person still in the closet, but close to exiting ("I'm sure Violet finds you attractive, seductive, and alluring, Monica. But give it a few weeks—she's still a tad confused").

DIGITAL QUEER Gay computer fanatic.

DOOR'S AJAR One who is very close to coming out of the closet ("Eva, that new girl at work is cute *and* I hear her door's ajar").

DRIVES ON THE OTHER SIDE OF THE ROAD
Lesbian/gay, and not necessarily from England.

FQA Future queen of America; a royally effeminate, regally prissy gay guy who has not discovered his own sexual orientation yet, even though one quick glance in the mirror would solve that problem.

FAG HAG Derogatory term for heterosexual female with almost exclusively gay circle of friends; often trendy in dress and manners and always seen on the dance floor at gay bars.

FAMILY Gay ("I just found out my boss was family . . . and to think I have talked about hockey scores for the past six months to throw him off!"). *Also:* family member.

FISH Forget the guppies and sea bass; derogatory term for female. It's an olfactory organ thing.

FRUITFLY Pesky, straight female who hangs around gay guys ("Grab the Raid! Anastasia, the quintessential fruit fly, is buzzing our way!").

GAY Used since the 1920s by homosexual women and men as an alternative to clinical term *homosexual,* but most popular since the 1960s. In the 1990s used more to describe homosexual men, versus homosexual women who often prefer the term *lesbian.*

GUPPIE Gay urban professional ("I'd sure like to have that Guppie in the Armani suit in my tank!").

GUPPIES
(GAY URBAN PROFESSIONALS)

HETEROASSUMPTIVE Assuming someone is heterosexual. *Also:* homoassumptive (assuming someone is homosexual).

HETEROFLEXIBLE Bisexual, or at least open to sexual experimentation.

HETEROSEXUAL One attracted to the opposite sex; straight. First used in the 1890s in American medical journals.

HOMOSEXUAL Man who chooses man/woman who chooses woman as a sexual, emotional, and psychological target of opportunity. Coined by Hungarian physician Karoly Maria Benkert in 1869 in letter to Prussian minister of justice, calling for repeal of laws persecuting homosexuals.

IN THE CLOSET Lesbian/gay people who keep their sexual orientation secret from either themselves, some people, or all people. *Also:* closeted.

JOANN Someone who is bisexual; a name that is both male and female ("So who will it be tonight, JoAnn? The stud with the tight CK jeans or his top-heavy friend in the leather bustier?").

LAVENDER LEAGUE Lesbian/gay ("Virginia can help you pick out a tool set . . . she plays for the lavender league"). Besides the more well-known pink, lavender is often associated with homosexuality.

LESBIGAY All-encompassing term for lesbian, gay, and bisexual people.

NEAR QUEER One who is nearly out of the closet.

ON THE TEAM Lesbian or gay person; one who is a member of Team Homo. *Also:* batting for the other team, a member of the pink team/triangle team, and so forth.

ONE OF US The few. The proud. The homosexuals. ("Please! I knew years ago that Melissa Etheridge was one of us.")

OUT Lesbian/gay person whose sexual orientation is no secret to friends and family.

OUTING Controversial practice of exposing closeted lesbian/gay individuals, especially well-known people, as a means of educating the public about the diversity of the homosexual community.

PANSEXUAL Someone who does anyone or anything at any time, anywhere (gay surfer term).

How much is this vase ma'am... um, I mean Sir... no, uh....

PAT

PAT Androgynous person. Origin: from gender-bending character on *Saturday Night Live*.

PINK POSSE Lesbian or gay people. If homosexuals had gangs, this would be their name. ("And for your initiation into the Pink Posse, François, you have to wear plaid *and* checks at the same time!"). Pink is often associated with lesbians and gay men because of the pink triangles used to identify homosexuals in World War II concentration camps.

PREFERS STUFFING INSTEAD OF POTATOES Gastronomic term for homosexual ("Meredith's engaged to a man? I thought she preferred stuffing instead of potatoes!").

QUEER Homosexual. Once derogatory, now often used by lesbians and gays in an effort to destigmatize the term.

SINGS IN THE CHOIR One who is part of the homosexual community; think of it as the Homo Tabernacle Choir.

For your initiation into the Pink Posse, François, you have to wear plaid and checks... at the SAME TIME!

PINK POSSE

STRAIGHT Heterosexual.

STRAIGHT BUT NOT NARROW Heterosexuals who wouldn't even think of discriminating on the basis of sexual orientation.

TV Transvestite; technical term for straight or gay cross-dresser (according to research, most transvestites are heterosexual men).

TACO Woman, or that part of a woman that is south of the border.

TRADE World War I–era name for heterosexual men who allowed gay men to have sex with them.

TUNED IN TO ANOTHER CHANNEL Lesbian/gay ("Sorry Rupert. Vivian may be beautiful, witty, and available, but I'm afraid she's tuned in to another channel.").

WANNABE Straight person who pretends to be homosexual ("Jasmine is the biggest wannabe, working that k.d. lang look at the bar, flirting with all the dykes, then going home to her husband").

WRECKED Lesbian/gay, especially glaringly so ("Danielle gave her girlfriend a huge, slobbery kiss, right in the middle of the food court at the mall! Now everybody knows she's wrecked!). *Also:* I wrecked Yves at the office Christmas party (let everyone know he was gay).

4

Shake Your
Groove Thangs

SEXUAL TERMINOLOGY

B.C. Before condoms. The era when, if it felt good, we did it.

BASKET Crotch area of a clothed man ("If his basket was any bigger he'd rip through those Levi's!").

BASKET

BED DEATH When the sexual hunger in a relationship evolves into a loss of appetite ("Of course Vera and Sylvia look sullen. Their relationship suffers from terminal bed death.").

BOOTY 1. Butt (as in "Shake, shake, shake; shake, shake, shake; shake your booty; shake your booty"). 2. Sex (as in "Rudy got some booty"). Origin: African-American.

BOTTOM 1. In the gay guy sexual realm, the partner who chooses passivity. 2. Gay guy who likes to be submissive.

BOX Crotch area of a clothed man ("nice butt, but no box"). *Also:* pushing box, meaning to arrange one's endowment in order to create the most impressive presentation.

BROOM IN A CAVE Performing anal sex with a partner who is a tad loose from much experience.

BUYSEXUAL When materialism steers the sex drive, as in "Buy me something and I'll be sexual."

CANYON YODELING Anal-oral contact.

CHANGE PURSE
Uncircumcised ("Imagine my surprise when he stepped out of the shower sporting a change purse!").

CHICKEN SNATCHI-TORI Having sex with a younger guy/gal (gay surfer term).

CHUBBY CHASER Those who choose their dates based on the adage "the more in the saddle, the better the straddle."

CLEAN KITCHEN A gay guy's freshly scrubbed and cologne-scented

BUYSEXUAL

CHUBBY CHASER

genital region, usually in preparation for sexual activity ("Tonight is your fifth date with Hector, and knowing your sexual track record, make sure you have a clean kitchen before you pick him up").

COCKRING One ring you probably won't find at your local jewelers; metal or leather ring placed around base of male genitalia to keep penis at attention.

COOTER Vagina. Whether this derives from the dark grey duck of the same name is anyone's guess.

CRUISE People-watching with a purpose; the gay guy act of wandering the bar, mall, or wherever to see if another guy locks eyes with you.

CUT Circumcised.

DAISY CHAIN Orgy activity in which a person services another person, who is servicing another person, and so on. An adult film standard.

DENTAL DAM Square of latex used by both males and females for protection during oral sex.

DO To have sex with ("I'd do her in a minute!").

DOOR WHORE A date who is in and out of your door for one thing only; sort of like Avon calling, but offers skin rather than Skin So Soft.

DOOR WHORE

GAG REFLEX TEST 1950s study that purported to identify gay men; the test supposedly

Let me know when you feel the tongue depressor.

showed that homosexuals did not show a gag reflex when a tongue depressor was put down their throat. Gag me with a spoon!

GAG REFLEX TEST

GAY FOR PAY Heterosexual hustler who will sleep with men . . . if the price is right!

GERONTOPHILE Younger person who is enamored of much, much older folks. *See* SUGAR DADDY in chapter 6.

GET LUCKY To make a love/lust connection.

GLORY HOLE Insert Peg A into Slot B; a hole in the wall into which (1) a guy inserts his penis to enjoy anonymous oral sex, or (2) a guy performs anonymous oral sex on a penis that appears through the hole. Glory, glory, hallelujah!

GREEK Anal-oriented sexual activity.

GROWER, NOT A SHOW-ER The "big things come in small packages" concept; a penis that becomes surprisingly grandiose when erect.

HOLE PATROL Looking for lust in all the right places.

HONEY POT The private parts of a woman ("Jude's new nickname is Winnie the Pooh because she's always in search of the next honey pot!").

HOT 1. Describes someone who is really, really, *really* attractive. 2. Describes something with awesome qualities ("She was working this hot little spandex number last night").

HUNG Stallionlike penis ("I screamed like a woman when he disrobed . . . he was hung like a horse!"). Hi-ho, Silver, away!

HUNG LIKE A DOUGHNUT One who could nickname his penis "inchworm."

HUNK Beefcake guy, handsome and muscled. *Also:* hunky.

HUSTLER A penny for your thoughts, fifty bucks for the rest of you; when you pay to play. After sex, the first words you hear won't be "Was it good for you?" but "Cash, check, or credit card?"

IN LUST Sort of like "in love," but without the love part; complete sexual infatuation.

KEPT One who is "provided for" by another individual in exchange for sex/companionship/sex. *See* SUGAR DADDY in chapter 6.

KOSHER MEAT Circumcised penis. Oy vey!

LUBE Lubricant. For latex condoms, petroleum jelly is a no-no, but Astro-Glide makes you go-go.

MACKIN' Gay surfer term for kissing ("How did Genevieve move up to manager? She was mackin' the boss's butt! That's how!").

MEAT Penis ("He's got a piece of meat not even a vegetarian would turn down!").

OREO Areola.

PACKAGE Crotch area of a clothed man. P.S. Good things *do* come in small packages. *See* GROWER, NOT A SHOW-ER.

THE PARK IS CLOSED What one says to his or her partner upon reaching climax, especially after intercourse.

PETER METER Imaginary gauge used by gay guys for measuring sexual attraction ("That stud scores a major reading on the ol' peter meter").

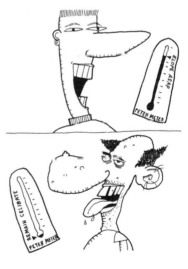

PETER METER

POGUE World War I–era term for men who were bottoms.

POPPERS Amyl nitrate, often sniffed

during 1970s and 1980s in gay bars or during sex, to get an immediate high. Can also be used as video head cleaner or paint stripper.

PROTECTION A condom. *Also:* armor, balloon, diving suit, glove, latex, life jacket, party hat, raincoat, rubber, sheath, shield.

PRINCE ALBERT The kind of piercing they don't do at that little stand in the middle of the mall: a penis piercing. A royal pain in the pecker if you catch it in your zipper.

PUMP A not entirely romantic description of intercourse, but vivid for sure.

SOD Sleep-over date.

SAFER SEX Sex practices that reduce the risk of contracting sexually transmitted diseases, especially AIDS. Usually includes any practice that avoids the exchange of bodily fluids.

SAUSAGE Penis that's bigger than a frank.

SEX REASSIGNMENT The medical procedure by which a man becomes a woman or a woman becomes a man.

SIZE QUEEN Gay guy who prefers quantity rather than quality of men, especially as it relates to genital size.

SMOKE & POKE To smoke pot and have intercourse.

SMOOTH Hairless body, either naturally or with a little help from Nair/shaver.

SNATCH Vagina.

STUD Masculine, muscle-packed guy. Usually removes his shirt on the dance floor (Can you blame him?).

Rather than alphabetizing, Seth finds another method to organize his old boyfriends.

2-4-6-8...who do we appreciate

LITTLE BLACK BOOK

SIZE QUEEN

SWIMMER'S BUILD Describes smooth, toned, hairless male body. Depilatories often play a role in this look. *Opposite:* bear.

THO Titty hard-on; when lesbians get a woody.

TOOL No gay male home is complete without a couple: male sex organs. Home improvement, indeed! *Also:* rusty tool (sex drought), snap-on tool (dildo used by lesbians).

TOP In the gay male sexual realm, the partner who prefers to be the aggressor. *Opposite:* bottom.

TREASURE TRAIL Line of hair leading from a guy's belly button to regions south. *Also:* trail of paradise.

TRICK 1. The object of a one-night stand ("I thought that was Gerard's boyfriend, but it was just a trick"). 2. The act of committing a one-night stand ("Don't act like you're just getting home from your morning jog . . . you tricked last night, didn't you!").

TRIXIE One who participates in numerous tricks/one-night stands.

TWO-WAY ARTISTS Term used during World War I for men who enjoyed being top or bottom.

UNCUT Uncircumcised. Often considered a desirable quality in the United States because of its rarity.

WHISKER BISCUIT The kind of biscuit Pillsbury doesn't make; a vagina. Pop-n-fresh good!

5

So, Do You Come Here Often?

LOCATION TERMINOLOGY

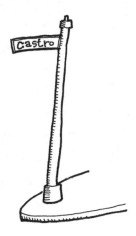

BSOC Be seen on Castro; dated San Francisco term suggesting that you must be seen at least once a week on Castro Street.

CAMP Place where lesbian/gay teens hang out, especially coffee houses ("I told my mom I was going to meet some guys at camp tonight, and she gave me marshmallows to roast").

COMMUNITY CENTER Social/educational/political headquarters for lesbian and gay people in their city or town.

And this is my roommate Alina's bedroom...

APRIL 1988

FAKE ROOM

FAKE ROOM Pretend bedroom in a lesbian/gay couple's home where, in order to fool unsuspecting heterosexuals, one partner supposedly sleeps.

FRUIT STAND Where the boys are; any locale ripe with gay guys.

GAY GHETTO Any of a number of neighborhoods in large cities with an almost exclusively lesbian/ gay population (South Beach in Miami, Boytown in Chicago, Dupont Circle in DC, West Hollywood near Los Angeles, Chelsea or the West Village in New York City, Montrose in Houston, etc.).

GAY-LERIA Mall with fags-a-plenty (From "galleria," standard name for sassy malls across America).

HARVEY MILK HIGH SCHOOL High school in New York City, primarily for lesbian and gay youth, run by the Hetrick-Martin Institute. Named for gay San Francisco city councilman assassinated in 1978.

HETRICK-MARTIN IN-STITUTE Private, nonprofit organization that provides many services for lesbian and gay youth (phone: 212/633-8920).

HOMO DEPOT Nickname for the often cruisy, always stud/lesbian-filled hardware superstore Home Depot. Who knew tool shopping could be so fun?

HOMO DEPOT

L & W BAR Leather/western bar. Git along little dogey!

LESBOS Greek isle and birthplace of Sappho, female poet who extolled the quality of love between women.

PANSY LAND Anyplace where the queens are blooming.

P-TOWN Provincetown, MA, gay resort mecca. Others include Key West, FL; Fire Island, NY; Rehoboth Beach, DE; Palm Springs, CA.

QUEER ONE Nickname for quirky, queer-favorite furnishings chain Pier One Imports.

RUTH ANN'S Rest area where clandestine sex occurs in the bushes or restrooms, as in "He may have a wife, but I hear he visits Ruth Ann's for a quickie every weekend."

THE SLIDE 1940s term for an establishment where male cross-dressers mingled.

SODOM AND GOMORRAH Towns in a biblical passage often cited to condemn homosexuals.

The story is not about sexual perversion/homosexual practice but about inhospitality (Luke 10:10–13) and failure to take care of the poor (Ezekiel 16:49–50). Amen!

STONEWALL INN Gay bar in Greenwich Village where on June 28, 1969, patrons fought back against police harassment; a turning point for the national gay rights movement.

THE SWISH ALPS Hollywood Hills, California. Yodel-lady-hoo!

6

7 Brides for 7 Sisters/ 7 Grooms for 7 Brothers

RELATIONSHIP TERMINOLOGY

Let me introduce you to Jane, my roommate of 19 years...

BETTER HALF Endearing but self-deprecating term describing your partner in a lesbian/gay relationship.

BOYFRIEND Term used to describe your partner in a gay male relationship.

COMMITMENT CEREMONY Nonlegal ceremony in which a lesbian or gay couple, in the company of family and friends, declare their vows and love for each other. Sometimes modeled after heterosexual weddings, complete with tiered wedding cake topped with either two grooms or two brides. *Also:* union or marriage ceremony.

DOMESTIC PARTNERSHIP Legal document offered by some cities to unmarried couples, but is largely symbolic and not equal to a marriage certificate.

FUSION When lesbians/gay men in a relationship nearly fuse into one person, losing all sense of individuality ("Did Sherie used to be the funny one and Yvonne the quiet one? It's so hard to remember since they experienced fusion.").

GAYBEE BOOM Gay parenting boom of the 1990s made possible through artificial insemination and adoption.

GIRLFRIEND Term of endearment between partners in a lesbian relationship.

HUSBAND Term of affection for a partner in a long-term, gay guy relationship.

LIFE PARTNER What some lesbians/gay people call their mates, though a tad new age–sounding for some.

LONGTIME COMPANION Obituary-speak for homosexual partner.

LOVER Partner description in lesbian/gay relationship; a bit too romance novelish sounding for many.

This is my **girlfriend**...well, it's a bit more than that -- this is my **lover**...actually that sounds a tad soap opera-ish -- this is my **partner**...h-m-m, that's sorta business sounding...

GIRLFRIEND/LOVER/ET AL.

MARRIED Describes lesbian or gay couple in committed relationship.

PNB Potential new boyfriend ("The gay pride parade was just teeming with PNBs!").

PARTNER Square dancing term that some lesbian/gay people use to describe their mate. Allemande left, girlfriend!

Let me introduce you to Jane, my roommate of 19 years...

ROOMMATE

ROOMMATE Non-affectionate euphemism for lesbian/gay partner, usually used when addressing straight people with whom your sexuality is secret ("Have you met Dominique, my roommate of 16 years who shares my one-bedroom home?").

SIGNIFICANT OTHER Descriptive but technical term describing one partner in a lesbian/gay couple. *Also:* S.O.

SUGAR DADDY Older gay guy who provides the cash to a younger guy who provides . . . whatever comes up. *Also:* sugar mama (lesbian version).

WIFE Slang for one partner of a lesbian/gay couple.

7

Talk the Talk

PHRASES AND ACRONYMS

Campy (gay guy style)

Campy (lesbian style)

And this fabulous "Dogs Playing Poker" painting is my latest art acquisition...

AESTHETICALLY IMPAIRED

ADF Alcohol distortion factor; the unique quality of alcohol that alters your ability to judge people, places, and things ("Nigel nearly went home with that guy who looked like an axe murderer . . . it had to be the ADF in effect").

AESTHETICALLY IMPAIRED When you think multicolored, sculptured shag carpeting should make a comeback.

ATTITUDE Disposition, usually snippy/bitchy, that one expresses either verbally or nonverbally ("Miss Thing over there can only throw attitude when she's sporting Versace").

BACK IN YOUR KENNEL! Command to control an unruly, vicious person (especially a queen).

BA-GOCK! Expression of surprise, often sung in a high-pitched voice like a chicken (gay surfer term).

BRICKWALL Southern term for "Shut the hell up and get out of my face!" used in conjunction with the "stop" hand gesture ("I've heard enough Skyler! Brickwall!). The counter move to brickwall is called "Free Willy." If you are brickwalled, immediately make your hand jump over the person's "stop" hand gesture and say "Free Willy, baby!" (as in "I'll say what I want, when I want!").

BUTCH IN THE STREETS, FEMME IN THE SHEETS Lesbian/gay guy who works the tough image in public, but is always on the bottom at home.

BUTCH IT UP To act more masculine, often to avoid getting beaten up ("I suggest you butch it up, girl. That big pickup truck with the gun racks next to us is full of mean-looking rednecks and they're looking your way.").

BUZZ KILL Gay surfer term for something that immediately cancels a good mood ("The date was fabulous until he started talking about genital warts . . . what a buzz kill").

CBC Cracker barrel crowd; white, rural-oriented individuals who probably don't belong to the Rainbow Coalition. Yeehaw! The lard-fried okra is the special of the day!

Campy (gay guy style)

CAMPY Amusing, outlandish, kitschy, overly theatrical.

Campy (lesbian style)

Has nothing whatsoever to do with camping in the wilderness, which of course would relate only to lesbians. Campy things include drag Tupperware parties and movies starring Divine.

CAN YOU SAY ... Catty prelude to a put-down (after dealing with a crabby salesperson, you say to your friend, "Can you say personality challenged?").

CAT FIGHT When queens get in a tiff. Watch the claws, girls!

CHATTY CATHY A babbler ("Head toward the hors d'oeuvres. Here comes that chatty cathy from the gym."). Derives from 1960s and 1970s doll of the same name that rambled incessantly when you pulled her string.

CLOCK To determine that a person is lesbian or gay ("Stop with that Patsy Cline imitation or those rednecks over there are going to clock you!").

CUH-CHING Cash register sound effect denoting something pricy, often used in sarcastic terms ("Nice little handbag, Haley. Cuh-CHING!").

DEADER THAN DISCO Describes anything currently out of vogue ("Anders did his whole salon in harvest gold and burnt orange . . . that color scheme is deader than disco").

DELISH Delicious ("That hunk in the tight tee is delish!").

DISH DIRT Share gossip ("Girl, we dished so much dirt I had to take a bubble bath!").

DYKE ALERT Alerting your companion that a lesbian is nearby; can be accomplished by either saying "dyke alert" quietly, or by making a previously agreed upon code sound. *Also:* fag alert.

EC Sounds like "easy"; as in "take it easy" ("EC with that snippy attitude, Celeste. You're going to get in a cat fight!").

EMOTIONAL ATM One who automatically keeps giving and giving in a relationship; no service charge required.

(Sob...HOW could you dump me (sob)... you broke my heart right in two (sob)...

EMOTIONAL ROADKILL

EMOTIONAL ROAD-KILL Like a possum squished in the street by a careless driver, the sobbing heap dumped by a careless lover (gay surfer term).

FABULOUS The standard among all gay guy exclamatory clichés. Often pronounced as "faaaa-bulous!" with the number of A's directly corresponding to the fabulousness of the situation (that is, a sassy new "do" would be faaa-bulous, while front row seats at a Patti LaBelle concert would be faaaaaa-bulous). *Also:* fabulicious (looks good and tastes great!).

FESTIVE Anything with partylike flavor ("Those rainbow-colored clogs are so festive!" or "Your exotic beer party was so festive!"). A major component of a queen's vocabulary.

FIERCE Better than fabulous (Gaultier's fall line is fierce!").

FLAWLESS Almost fierce, but often used sarcastically ("Flawless apartment, Sydney. Have you named the cockroaches yet?").

FOR DAYS Exaggeration ("I thought I was a little overweight, but Aida's got thighs for days!").

FRAPPE LA RUE Distorted French phrase for "hit the road"; to get loose and crazy and carefree.

GNC Geographically not compatible; a possible new boyfriend or girlfriend who lives just too damn far away from you.

GET OVER YOU! Said to a person who believes they are much more important/attractive/etc. than they really are.

GOIN' THROUGH CHANGES Queen talk for upset ("Hide the Waterford. Stefan is goin' through changes again.").

GO ON GIRL! Gay guy term that says, "I'm impressed!" ("You got those Gucci loafers on sale? Go on girl!") *Also:* You go girl. Origin: African American.

GRAB A RAIL! Get control of yourself! ("Grab a rail, girl! You're going to have a nervous breakdown!").

HMA Hot man alert; signal to those around you that a good-looking guy is near. *Also:* HWA for hot woman alert.

HAMSTER WHEEL Gay surfer term that describes one who is trapped in a cycle of confusion, pity, or self-doubt ("Ramona, stop obsessing about your sorry love life! Get off your hamster wheel and get a date!").

HEL-LO! All-purpose interjection that might mean "Oh my God," "Wake up idiot," or "Get a life" ("Lamont thought risotto was a country . . . Hel-LO!").

HISSY FIT A fag-oriented tantrum.

HIT ME ON THE HEAD Slang for "page me" (gay surfer term).

HOMOTION Any stereotypical, effeminate movement, like a loose wrist or swishy walk ("Lose the homotions, Guy, we're in a straight bar").

HONEY, I'M HOMO! Affectionate greeting said by someone to his or her partner upon returning home.

IG To snub ("Don't ig me, Miss Thing. You're not important enough.").

LET ME INTRODUCE YOU TO MR. CLICK Said just prior to hanging up on someone.

MARTHA

MARTHA As in Martha Stewart ("Your table setting is so Martha!").

NEWSY AND NOW Something so current it screams for attention ("I love that new Armani Exchange store, Talbot. Everything is so newsy and now!").

-ORAMA

-ORAMA Suffix that turns plain old words into a bonanza ("Look at those women by the pool . . . boobo-rama!"). Other examples: bouffantorama, crotchorama, polyes-terorama.

PECKY Describes guy with well-developed pectoral muscles ("Karsten's not much in the conversation department, but girl is he pecky!").

PORTABLE LIE A falsehood that conveniently travels with someone wherever he or she goes ("Lindley tells everyone he's a model . . . he's been toting that portable lie around for years").

PRESH Precious. Term of endearment from a queen ("Listen presh, with all due respect, lose that Old Spice cologne or people will think you're a straight boy!").

READ YOUR BEADS Tell someone off ("If he lost my Abba CD, I'm gonna read his beads!").

SAS Sudden accent syndrome; one who mysteriously effects a foreign accent in midconversation (gay surfer term).

SASSY Describes gay guy who is extra hip with a bit of attitude.

SAS

SE DICE NADA, SE HACE TODO Say nothing, do everything; customary approach to homosexuality in Latin America and the Caribbean.

SINCE TONIGHT IS ALL ABOUT YOU Sarcastic comment as in, "No, really, none of us mind leaving the Barbra Streisand concert early since you have to get up early for a hair appointment . . . I mean, since tonight is all about you . . ."

STRAIGHTENING UP
THE HOUSE

STRAIGHTENING UP THE HOUSE Practice of removing all signs of homosexuality from your abode in preparation for a visit from straight people with whom your sexuality is a secret. Coined by recording artists Romanovsky and Phillips in the song of the same name.

THIS IS AN A-B CONVERSATION . . . WHY DON'T YOU C YOUR WAY OUT Snippy, geometrylike response used when a third party interrupts your conversation.

TIRED A person/style with an expired freshness date ("That tired old drag queen has worked that Tina Turner look one decade too long").

TO DIE FOR When something is so desirable you would trade your life for it ("That Ralph Lauren dust ruffle is to die for!").

TOUCH YOU! Gay exclamation that expresses how impressed you are with someone ("You won the wet underwear contest at the bar last night? Well, touch you!").

TRÈS All-purpose French adjective for "very" ("That headband she's wearing is très *Flashdance!*").

TWO SNAPS UP Ratings system used by faux gay movie reviewers on old Fox comedy show *In Living Color*. One snap = fair, two snaps = good, etc. Snap motion is executed with a quick flick of the wrist back over the shoulder.

WE'RE GOING TO HAVE A GAY TIME TONIGHT Supposed signal used by lesbians in World War II to identify each other. *Also:* Are you in the mood?

WONDERFUL Interjection overused by gay guys ("That new apricot face scrub is *wonderful!* Milan is *wonderful!* That new Quentin Tarantino movie is *wonderful!*").

WORKING MY LAST GAY NERVE Aggravating/irritating someone ("Honey, make a decision! You are working my last gay nerve!").

WORK IT Use everything you have to impress. Popularized in song by entertainer/drag queen RuPaul.

ZIRCON One who puts on haughty airs despite the fact that he or she doesn't have a pot to piss in ("Don't let that zircon Sofia give you attitude—she's got 'Karl Lagerfeld for Chanel' taste and a 'Jaclyn Smith for Kmart' budget"). Derives from the manmade diamond look-alike cubic zirconia.

8

Fashion Before Comfort/ Comfort Before Fashion

APPEARANCE

TERMINOLOGY

Lori's gaydar is not quite as subtle nor innate as she thinks it is.

BETTY BOUFFANT
Someone with big hair ("I was going to take the top down on my Miata, but the Betty Bouffants in the back seat feared for their hair").

BETTY BOUFFANT

BIG HAIR A coiffure with altitude; hairstyles with extra, extra body and lots of hair spray.

BOOGER An unattractive person ("Did Lamont break up with his boyfriend? I just saw him at the mall with the biggest booger!").

BUSY Complicated, fussy ("I know Todd Oldham showed that in his winter line, but your plaid slacks and striped shirt are bordering on busy, Felipe").

CALVINS Clingy undies with sexual orientation–challenged Calvin Klein's name stitched around the waistband.

Is that Tom Cruise over there?

JUST DO ME

DDW

CRAPLIQUÉ Sounds like "appliqué"; tacky T-shirts and sweatshirts with poofy paint and shiny stuff all over.

DDW Distance does wonders. The optical illusion that a person is great-looking from afar; this is disproved upon closer inspection. *Also:* DDF (distance distortion factor).

DO Hairdo ("This blustery wind is wreaking havoc on my new do").

EYE CANDY Person who is so cute it makes your fillings hurt (gay surfer term).

FEATURE To display or exhibit a new outfit, hairstyle, piece of jewelry, etc. (I know you won't want to be seen with Xavier at the club tonight. He's featuring a hairdo from hell.").

FROCK 1. A dress. 2. Any outfit, especially a new one ("Why, look at the new frock Antonio has on. He must be on a manhunt.").

Lori's gaydar is not quite as subtle nor innate as she thinks it is.

GAYDAR

GAYDAR The innate ability possessed by most lesbians and gays, as well as some straight people, to determine if people are homosexual by their mere presence (but not necessarily based on their appearance). It's a gay thing.

GENDER BENDER One whose looks defy sex-typing, often prompting comments like, "Is that a cute guy or a boyish-looking lesbian over by the bar?"

HAIR-DON'T When a hairdo doesn't do it.

IRON DEFICIENT When you look like you slept in the clothes you are wearing; a spray-starch–challenged individual.

LEATHER MAN/CHICK Gay guy or lesbian with affinity for rawhide (not the TV series); often into rougher sex.

LEVI'S 501 JEANS The jean of choice for many gay guys. Those metal buttons accentuating the fly make for a perfect presentation of your package. Plus you can't get your thing caught in the zipper.

NTL No tan line ("I saw Jose at the gym . . . NTL!").

POSER One who strikes a model stance (the "My-Appearance-Is-My-Best-Feature" look), especially in a gay bar, in hopes of attracting attention.

PRETTY BOY Opposite of the butch look; a guy so lovely that you think, "Lord he'd look good in drag."

RED NECKTIE The "badge" of gay guys in the early 20th century.

ROOSTER CUT Hairstyle of some butch lesbians, short on sides, long in back, spiky on top. A real cockle doodle DO.

SCARE-DO A hairstyle that frightens young children and the elderly.

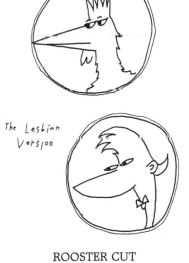

The Original

The Lesbian Version

ROOSTER CUT

SCARE-ELLA Unattractive person ("That Sun-In fried my hair . . . guess I'll be working that scare-ella look tonight").

SEA HAG

SEA HAG Former beach bunny turned bitchy, nasty, and crusty from the sun's harmful rays (gay surfer term).

STEROID QUEEN Gay guy with artificially enhanced musculature, usually at the expense of his intelligence and penis size.

STRAIGHT-ACTING Often erroneously used to describe a masculine gay guy. As we all know, "straight" does not always equal "masculine" or "desirable" (for example, Tiny Tim, Charles Manson).

STUD MUFFIN Male or female hunk.

TPT Trailer park trash; undesirable ("What do I think about your new boyfriend? Well, he drives a rusty '86 Camaro and doesn't have a job. That spells TPT."). *Also:* WT (white trash), BT (black trash), LT (Latin trash).

TRAUMA Dramatic suffix used by gay guys when experiencing difficulty getting ready ("I'll never be on time to the play! I'm having a _____ trauma!" Fill in the blank: hair, shoe, cologne, etc.).

VSS Visible sweat stains ("Chanel suit or not, Constance blew that interview because of VSS").

Wardrobe Trauma

TRAUMA

9

I Love a Parade

ENTERTAINMENT
TERMINOLOGY

BAR HAG

AFTER-HOURS CLUB
Where bar hags go when
the clubs close at dawn.

BAR HAG One who fre-
quents gay bars, drinks
a lot, and knows bar-
tenders by name.

BLACK CAT San Francisco bar that was one of the
first exclusively gay bars (1940s) in the United
States. *Also:* Bradley's in Hollywood, Mary's
Tavern in Denver. Lesbian bars include the If

Club in Los Angeles and Mona's in San Francisco.

CIRCUIT The festively hectic schedule of large-scale homosexually oriented parties that occur throughout the United States, from Key West to Palm Springs.

DISCO NAP Late afternoon beauty rest in preparation for a late night on the town.

GAY BAR Centerpiece of many gay social scenes; where lesbian/gay people congregate to drink, dance, and cruise in a (relatively) safe atmosphere.

GAY CRUISE Chartered cruise specifically targeted for lesbian and gay travelers. And Kathy Lee thought *she* was queen of the sea!

GAY SKATE Evening set aside at skating rink for homos on wheels.

GAYLA Any predominantly lesbian/gay social event.

HIGH NRG High-energy dance music featured at most gay bars; fast, furious, relentless, and oh, oh, oh, so repetitive.

INFINITY MIX Version of a club song that seems to never end; don't head to the floor when you hear these songs unless you really like your dance partner, have gone to the bathroom recently, and have strong arches.

JUDY, BETTE, LIZA, ET AL. Judy Garland, Bette Davis/Bette Midler, and Liza Minnelli; female stars revered by many gay guys. *Also:* Joan Crawford, Barbra Streisand, and Marilyn Monroe.

MELISSA, LILY, K.D., ET AL. Melissa Etheridge, Lily Tomlin, and k.d. lang; performers revered by many lesbians. *Also:* Ellen DeGeneres, Paula Poundstone, and Catherine Deneuve.

MUSIC FESTIVAL No boys allowed! All-lesbian gathering with all lesbian entertainment . . . a lesborama.

PETTING ZOO Male strip clubs in Washington, DC, and other major cities where you can pet the wildlife. Old MacDonald never had a farm like this! E-I-E-I-O-Boy!

POT LUCK DINNER What lesbians often host when their entertaining skills are lacking, or what gay guys host if Martha Stewart features one in her magazine that month.

PRIDE PARADE Held in major cities during Gay Pride month (June).

S & M BAR Stand and model bar; gay club loaded with studs, hunks, and pretty boys who strike a pose.

TEA DANCE An excuse to visit a gay bar before it gets dark outside; usually when a bar hosts a Sunday afternoon soiree.

VOGUE Dance that mimics modeling poses. Unveiled to the masses by Madonna in song of the same name.

WHITE PARTY Popular, almost tired, theme party requiring all white attire; often underwear oriented (for example, Miami's White Party at the Italian Renaissance estate Vizcaya).

10

J. Edgar Hoover Slept Here

POLITICAL, SOCIAL, AND
HISTORICAL TERMINOLOGY

AFFIRMATION Name shared by the national organizations for gay Methodists and gay Mormons.

BLUE DISCHARGES World War II discharge papers for homosexuals. The gay man or lesbian was labeled as an "undesirable," but the discharge was neither dishonorable nor honorable.

BOSTON MARRIAGES Intimate lesbian love relationships in the early 1900s.

BUN WOMAN Holier-than-thou type of woman who rallies against lesbian/gay people. Origin:

You fags are going to burn in **HELL**, you **EVIL** scum-sucking slimeballs! Don't you read the Bible?

ADAM&EVE
NOT
ADAM&STEVE

BIBLE JUDGE NOT

BUN WOMAN

From the hairstyle featuring a large sweet roll–looking bun. Think Anita Bryant.

CHICAGO SOCIETY FOR HUMAN RIGHTS

First gay rights group in the United States, founded by Henry Gerber and chartered by the state of Illinois in 1924.

CHILD MOLESTERS What antihomosexual organizations call gays and lesbians. In fact, according to a study by Children's Hospital in Denver in 1992, a heterosexual male is the most likely person to molest a child. His victim is most likely female, and often the molester is a family member.

DAUGHTERS OF BILITIS Lesbian organization founded in San Francisco in 1955 by Del Martin and Phyllis Lynn. Published newsletter *The Ladder* (1956–1972).

DIGNITY National organization of gay Roman Catholics.

DON'T ASK/DON'T TELL Clinton-era military policy regarding homosexuality—officials cannot ask questions about sexual orientation, and lesbian/gay service people cannot mention their orientation. A compromise between the military (who wanted all homosexuals discharged) and the gay community (who wanted no discrimination within the armed forces).

FREEDOM RINGS As pearls were to Jackie O., freedom rings are to lesbians and gay men; small, rainbow-colored aluminum rings strung on a chain and worn as a symbol of gay pride. Designed by David Spada.

GAI Gay American Indians; the first gay American Indian liberation organization was formed in 1975 in San Francisco.

GLAAD Gay and Lesbian Alliance Against Defamation.

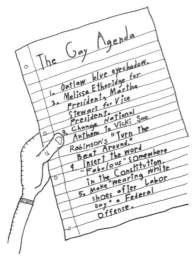

GAY AGENDA Propaganda-type term coined by the radical right (Pat Robertson, Jerry Falwell, et al.) describing a supposed set of antifamily goals created by gay and lesbian politicos.

GAY AGENDA

GAY BASH When ignorant heterosexuals beat up lesbian/gay people just because they are lesbian/gay people; offenders are often prosecuted under hate crime laws. *Also:* fag bash.

GAY-FRIENDLY Heterosexuals who treat lesbian/gay people like people.

GAY GAMES International Gay Athletic Games, first held in 1982 in San Francisco, and held every four years; founded by the late Dr. Tom Waddell (a U.S. Olympic decathlete in 1968).

GAY RIGHTS The belief that lesbian and gay people deserve the same rights as heterosexuals at federal, state, and local levels. Mistakenly referred to as "special rights" by the radical right. What's special about the legal protections straight Americans enjoy: protection from discrimination in employment, housing, public accommodation, etc.?

GAY RIGHTS

GILLETTE BLADES 1950s Hollywood-era term for actresses who cut both ways. *See* LAVENDER MARRIAGE.

HETEROSEXISM The ridiculous presumption of some straight people that the world runs in one gear: heterosexual mode. Example: applications that ask for marital status but include no provision for lesbian/gay couples.

HOMOEROTIC

HOMOEROTIC A feeling of desire for intimacy, admiration, or affection between members of the same sex (whereas the homosexual engages in the actual physical/sexual expression of those sentiments). Often used to describe advertisements, movies, etc., with lesbian/gay undertones, such as Calvin Klein underwear ads.

HOMOPHOBIA Irrational fear of lesbian/gay people that leads to bigotry and discrimination. *Also:* homophobe. Coined by author Wainwright Churchill in 1967 book *Homosexual Behavior Among Males. Also:* homophobe, 'phobe.

HOMOSEXUAL BUFFOONERY Game played by heterosexual soldiers in World War II barracks, where they jokingly acted out the role of "overt homosexuals" for laughs. Historical records show no incidents of gay men participating in heterosexual buffoonery, probably because the straight soldiers did such a good job of acting like buffoons on their own.

HOMOSOCIAL Heterosexual whose social circle is rife with lesbian/gay people ("No, Madeline is not a lesbian. She's simply homosocial.").

HUMANITARIAN COMMITTEE First homosexual rights organization. Founded in Germany in 1897. Who said lesbians and gays don't have a history?

DR. EVELYN HOOKER The Rosa Parks of the lesbian/gay movement. Heterosexual psychologist whose research in the 1950s led to the removal of homosexuality from the American Psychiatric Association's list of mental illnesses (1973). You go, girl!

INTEGRITY National organization for gay Episcopalians.

KINSEY SCALE Developed by Alfred Kinsey in the 1940s. Represents the range from exclusively

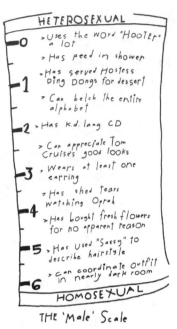

THE 'Male' Scale

HETEROSEXUAL

- 0
  - Uses the word "Hooter" a lot
  - Has peed in shower
  - Has served Hostess Ding Dongs for dessert
- 1
  - Can belch the entire alphabet
- 2
  - Has k.d. lang CD
  - Can appreciate Tom Cruise's good looks
  - Wears at least one earring
- 3
  - Has shed tears watching Oprah
- 4
  - Has bought fresh flowers for no apparent reason
- 5
  - Has used "Sassy" to describe hairstyle
  - Can coordinate outfit in nearly dark room
- 6

HOMOSEXUAL

heterosexual (zero) to exclusively homosexual (six). His books on human sexual behavior crushed the existing understanding of American sexual practices, proving that homosexuality was a far more common occurrence than once believed.

LAMBDA Greek letter used to symbolize gay liberation.

LAVENDER MARRIAGE Fake Hollywood marriages of the 1950s, when bisexual women married gay men.

LAVENDER MENACE 1960s term, coined by the National Organization of Women (NOW), to describe lesbians.

LEVITICUS 18:19–23, 20:10–16 Biblical citations often used to condemn homosexuals. Actually part of the Holiness Code of ancient Israel that not only prohibits homosexual acts but also wearing garments with two kinds of yarn, sex during a woman's menstrual period, and tattoos. Other citations often invoked include Deuteronomy 23:17, I Kings 14:24 and 22:46, and II Kings 23:7, but these simply forbid prostitution by women and men, not homosexuality.

LIFESTYLE Often used by homophobes to describe homosexual orientation ("that destructive gay lifestyle"). Based on urban, single nightlife led by some gay men in the 1970s. There is no definitive homosexual lifestyle, just as there is no one heterosexual lifestyle.

LOG CABIN CLUB National organization of gay republicans. No, honestly! This is not a typo!

MATTACHINE SOCIETY AND ONE, INC. Influential gay organizations originating in 1950s Los Angeles. Harry Hay, writer and activist, founded the Mattachine Society.

METROPOLITAN COMMUNITY CHURCH Christian church with primarily lesbian and gay church membership.

NGLTF National Gay and Lesbian Task Force.

NATIONAL COMING OUT DAY Celebrated October 11 (since 1988). Commemorates the 1987 gay and lesbian rights March on Washington, DC, and is a visibility campaign to put to rest the myths about homosexuals.

OPENLY GAY Heterosexual term meaning out of the closet. Often used in derogatory sense, as in "She should not be allowed to be an openly gay attorney."

PANSY RAID A panty raid gone bad; a gay bashing.

PASSIONISTS National organization for gay Southern Baptists.

P-FLAG Parents, Family & Friends of Lesbians and Gays; national support group. Phone: (202) 638-4200.

PINK PANTHERS/ANGELS Lesbian and gay street patrols that combat antigay attacks (New York, San Francisco, etc.).

PINK TRIANGLE An inverted triangle, first used in Nazi Germany to identify homosexuals in concentration camps. In the 1970s it became a symbol of pride for lesbian and gay people to commemorate those who died in the camps, and is still used as a symbol today.

PRIDE The feeling a lesbian/gay person has when not ashamed of his or her sexual orientation. *Also:* gay pride, Pride Parade.

RADICAL RIGHT Ultraconservative movement that mixes religion and politics and blatantly promotes discrimination toward lesbian and gay people. Includes the Christian Coalition, Concerned Women of America, Traditional Values Coalition, and Family Research Council. Once called "Religious Right," but they are hardly religious and rarely right about anything (especially relating to wardrobe, hair, or makeup application).

RAINBOW FLAG Symbol of gay pride, designed in 1978 by San Francisco resident Gilbert Baker. Often seen as a bumper sticker or as a banner in front of lesbian/gay homes/businesses.

RECRUITING The army does it. College football teams do it. Now antigay groups claim homosexuals have turned to recruiting too, looking for a few good men or a couple of tight ends. In real-

I'm Sergeant Sassy and this here's Lieutenant Lesbos...

RECRUITING

ity, one cannot change a straight person into a gay person any more than one can change a gay person into a straight person.

SACRED BAND OF THEBES Army of 150 pairs of homosexual lovers who vowed to stand/fall together. Unbeaten in battles for years, they were annihilated by Alexander the Great's father in 338 B.C.E. Be all that you can be, indeed!

SAGE Senior Action in a Gay Environment; national organization for elderly lesbian and gay people.

SALSA SOUL SISTERS Black lesbian group, started in 1974 by Luvenia Pinson, that launched a network of lesbians of color. Now called African Ancestral Lesbians United for Societal Change.

JOSE SARRIA First openly gay man to run for public office (1961, San Francisco).

SEWING CIRCLE Secret 1950s term for a group of famous Hollywood actresses who portrayed romantic heroines on screen but in private life were thought to be lesbian or bisexual. They included Joan Crawford, Greta Garbo, and Marlene Dietrich.

SEXUAL PREFERENCE Incorrect terminology for "sexual orientation."

SICK Infected with the AIDS virus.

SODOMY LAWS Laws in over half the states that make it illegal for lesbian and gay adults to "perform or submit to any sexual act involving the sex organs of one person and the mouth or anus of another." In most states these laws apply to both gay and straight people, but when these rarely used laws are enforced it is usually against homosexuals.

TEN PERCENT Commonly accepted figure representing percentage of population that is homosexual, developed by Alfred Kinsey in 1940. No definitive study has been done since that time.

VICE VERSA Earliest known U.S. periodical (1947) for lesbians, written by Lisa Ben.

THE WELL OF LONELINESS Published in 1928, a best-selling novel by lesbian author Radclyffe Hall that caused stirs across America for its accurate portrayal of the gay subculture.